The Second World War
Australian Home Front

Dana Walkens

MURRAY DAVID PUBLISHING AUSTRALIAN HISTORY SERIES

Contents

The Second World War

Australian Home Front

The term 'Home Front' refers to the civilian population of a nation at war. The activities of a wartime civilian population on the home front support the military fighting at 'The Front', that is, on the battlefield.

In the First World War (1914-1918), the battlefront was a world away from Australia in Europe and the Middle East. In the Second World War (1939-1945), Australian cities were attacked and major battles occurred not far away in Papua and New Guinea and South-east Asia. For this reason, the impact of the Second World War on the Australian home front was enormous. For the first time in Australia's history almost all of Australia's population was involved in a war.

The Second World War brought about considerable changes in Australian society, the economy and politics, some of which remain even today. The civil liberties of civilians were greatly reduced as the Government's powers escalated. Industry was affected as the need for war materials increased. The role of women changed significantly and conscription was introduced.

Government policies and many other aspects of the war meant that almost no-one in Australia was untouched by the effects of the Second World War.

TO THE WISE MAN . . .

Forewarned is Forearmed

SELF-HELP will be the watchword of wise householders this year. Australia's heavy food commitments, combined with drought conditions, impose a heavy strain on our food supplies. If water is available, get busy—

GROW YOUR OWN VEGETABLES

A leaflet encouraging the Australian public to help the war effort. (Australian War Memorial Negative Number RC00813)

The key word for Australian civilians during the Second World War was austerity. The Curtin Government launched a campaign of 'Austerity' in August 1942. This meant doing without, making do, living modestly and wasting nothing. Austerity encompassed many of the Government's regulations during wartime—rationing, limits on civil liberties, saving money to put into war loans, restrictions on leisure activities and production of luxury items. Prime Minister Curtin set an example with his simple way of life and long working hours which eventually took a toll on his health. He told Australians: 'Austerity calls for a pledge by the Australian people to strip every selfish comfortable habit, every luxurious impulse, every act, word and deed that retards the victory march'.

The Government promoted austerity in advertising campaigns featuring the 'Squander Bug'. The advertisements urged Australians to eliminate the Squander Bug, 'a friend of Hitler and Tojo', and 'save for victory' by investing in war loans.

The Effect of the War on Australian Politics and Government

The growth of the Government's power over the everyday life of Australians and the economy brought about the greatest changes on the Australian home front.

There was some hostility to the control the Government had over the population but generally Australians united to do everything they could for the war effort. In a similar fashion, there was greater co-operation between the major political parties as the politicians were united against a common enemy.

In 1940 an Advisory War Council was established to aid the Government in the war effort. It was based on a similar coalition Government set up in Britain during the war where all major political parties were represented.

The Increase in the Government's Powers

As a result of the Second World War the power and prestige of the Federal Government increased. The Federal Government

Governments in Australia during the Second World War

Australia's Wartime Prime Ministers

Robert Menzies, United Australia Party: Declaration of War, 3 September 1939–29 August 1941.
Arthur Fadden, United Australia Party: 29 August 1941–7 October 1941.
John Curtin, Australian Labor Party: 7 October 1941–5 July 1945. (Died in office).
Francis Forde, Australian Labor Party: 6 July 1945–13 July 1945.
Ben Chifley, Australian Labor Party: 13 July 1945–19 December 1945. (Chifley continued in office in peacetime until 19 December 1949).

took over roles that had previously been the State Governments' responsibilities as well as exercising direct control over the economy and society.

Most of the powers acquired by the Federal Government were due to the National Security Act which was passed on 9 September 1939. The Government could make laws by regulation without parliamentary intervention, which the Government claimed was necessary if urgent laws needed to be made. Parliament could discuss the laws if it was sitting, but parliament only sat for a few months each year. It basically overruled the Australian Constitution and parliament's powers and gave the Federal Government unprecedented powers.

The types of laws passed by the Government included:
Before the *National Security Act:*

- Censorship of mail
- Calling up men for service in the militia

Under the *National Security Act*:

- Greater censorship
- Forcing manufacturers to make essential war goods
- Interning those considered a security threat
- Manpower regulations
- Rationing
- Conscription
- Blackouts and brownouts
- Daylight saving

Royal Australian Air Force recruits queue at Victoria Barracks, Sydney, while waiting for transport to take them to their training station. 180 000 Australians volunteered to serve in the Air Force in a wide range of positions. 27 000 were trained as aircrew. (Australian War Memorial Negative Number 140357)

Volunteer Defence Corps members training prior to being issued with uniforms. In the early years of the war the Corps was raised and maintained by the RSL Later the Corps was handed over to Army control and was comprised of volunteers unfit for combat in the regular forces. (Australian War Memorial Negative Number: P02018.087)

Enlistment of women into the armed services
Issuing of identity cards
Banning some anti-war political parties

By the end of the war around 2 000 regulations had been made.

Censorship

The National Security Act granted the Government powers of censorship. Everything from newspapers to private mail was censored, as well as film and radio. Opposition to the war was not tolerated. A Department of Information, based loosely on the *British Ministry of Information*, was established on 4 September, 1939. It controlled censorship and propaganda.

Censorship was deemed necessary to protect military operations. Troop movements or military plans were never printed. The letters of military personnel in particular were targeted by the censor. Mail from suspected aliens, Australians known to be anti-war and other people in sensitive industries or places, was opened by the censor. The Government launched an advertising campaign warning of gossiping and careless talk that might be heard by enemy spies.

Censorship was also used to boost morale. Bad news of battles or other incidents were rarely reported. In August 1944 there was a breakout of over 1 000 Japanese prisoners of war at a camp in Cowra, New South Wales. Over 300 of these men were killed. News of the Cowra Breakout was censored in case it led to reprisals against Australian prisoners of war in Japanese camps. News of the bombing of Darwin was not reported and to this day the exact death toll is not known. Fights between US troops posted to Australia and Australians were not reported.

The Government also issued wartime propaganda to encourage a hatred of the enemy.

In April 1940 Communist newspapers were banned. In June newspapers were directed to print only war information supplied by the Government.

From 1943, Arthur Calwell was Minister for Information and he often had a political motivation for censoring the news. In mid-1944 two Sydney newspapers criticised the Government's censorship policy. Calwell's reaction was to

Sunday Telegraph

Vol. V. No. 23 Telephone: M2406 · SYDNEY, SUNDAY, APRIL 16, 1944 Registered at the G.P.O., Sydney, for transmission by post as a newspaper Price 3d

NAZI FLIGHT FROM SEBASTOPOL

Red armies link for final blow

SUNDAY TELEGRAPH SERVICE AND AAP

LONDON, Sat.—Two Russian armies have linked up for the final assault against Sebastopol, Crimean naval base.

With Red Army spearheads less than 16 miles from the city, the Germans are in full flight, abandoning guns and equipment.

Moscow radio said today: "The soil is burning under the feet of the brutal invader. The Germans run like rats in a trap."

Russian planes and warships are ceaselessly attacking German vessels attempting to evacuate troops from Sebastopol.

Germans massed on the beaches waiting to be picked up are meeting a relentless hail of bombs and cannonfire.

Correspondents say the Germans face an ordeal equalling, perhaps exceeding, that of the British Expeditionary Force which was evacuated from Dunkirk in June, 1940.

Russian dive-bombers, operating from newly captured bases in the Crimea, are blasting all roads along which the Germans are retreating to Sebastopol.

The Russian pilots, who pick out the fleeing German columns by the dust-clouds they create, are causing terrific traffic jams.

German soldiers are leaving their vehicles, throwing away their rifles, and fleeing on foot in hope of reaching Sebastopol in time to be evacuated.

Slaughter Expected

Before moving on from Simferopol (Crimean capital), captured yesterday, General Tolbukhin's troops knelt in the city square and swore complete liberation of the Crimea by hurling the Germans into the sea.

Moscow radio has broadcast an order to the Russian Black Sea Fleet not to let the Germans escape.

British United Press Moscow correspondent says once Sebastopol falls it will be wholesale slaughter.

More than 31,000 Germans and Rumanians have been captured, and only the south-west tip of the Crimea remains in enemy hands.

At one point the Russians have cut off a large group of Germans and Rumanians.

Yesterday the Russians, reinforced with tanks and mechanised infantry, swept the enemy rearguard from 500 towns and villages.

At least one division was annihilated.

A Moscow communique says: "The enemy in the Crimea is retreating everywhere in panic, abandoning not only arms, equipment, and transport, but even personal belongings, greatcoats, helmets, gasmasks, and kitbags."

Prisoners say many senior German and Rumanian officers have already left the Crimea by plane for Rumania.

A captured German commander told the Russians: "Your tanks have turned us into a flock of sheep."

General Tolbukhin's army, advancing from the north, linked up with General Yeremenko's forces, driving from the east, at a point 16 miles north-east of Sebastopol, yesterday.

To meet Yeremenko's army, Tolbukhin marched his men 25 miles over a mountain range.

Reuter's Moscow correspondent says: "General Yeremenko's men, striking along the famous marine drive in the southern Crimea, are finding German dead in fields, among beds of spring flowers, and in orchards where fruit and blossom have been slashed by gunfire."

Capture of the Crimea will free Tolbukhin and Yeremenko's armies for operations in Rumania, already deeply penetrated by Marshal Koniev's Second Ukrainian Army and Marshal Zhukov's First Ukrainian Army.

General Malinkovsky's Third Ukrainian Army, which last Monday captured the Black Sea port of Odessa, is mopping up German forces near the mouth of the Dniester River (Bessarabian border).

The Russians are preparing Odessa as a base for a renewed thrust into Rumania.

Counter In Poland

Daily Express military correspondent says the Germans are about to launch a large-scale counter-offensive in south-east Poland, between the Pripet Marshes and the upper Dniester River.

Big troop concentrations have been seen moving from the rear areas, and deploying into battle positions.

See Time, page 11.

Laugh with Beachcomber. Page 24

MINDING BABIES holds no terrors for 17-year-old Ron Ruddy, process worker, of Potts Point, photographed yesterday with four of the seven babies allocated to his care at the Belhaven Wartime Baby Home. Ruddy volunteered to work at the home in response to an appeal for spare-time helpers. "I'd like to do it every day," he said.

Main Burma clash to come

Sunday Telegraph Service and AAP

LONDON, Sat. — Decisive fighting on the India-Burma front is still to come, the B.B.C. says.

A B.B.C. reporter in eastern India says the main clash will occur north of Kohima where the Japanese are in "the greatest strength."

Kohima is 60 miles north of Imphal, capital of Manipur State, and is 46 miles from the railway supplying Allied forces on the Indian and North Burma fronts.

British and Indian troops have repelled several Japanese attempts to take Kohima in the last week.

Another Japanese force from Burma has by-passed Imphal to the south.

See Time, page 11.

YOUTHS REPRIEVED FROM DEATH AFTER LAST MEAL

SUNDAY TELEGRAPH SERVICE

NEW YORK, Sat.—After eating what they believed was their last meal, two youths were saved from the electric chair today by last-minute reprieve.

Chief item in the meal was their favorite dish, fried chicken.

The youths are Gordon Cooke, 20, and Winston Sealy, 22, convicted of

A reprieve to May 4 has been granted by New York Governor Dewey, pending arguments for new trials based on fresh evidence.

Two other youths awaiting execution were granted reprieve to May 4 for

The Sydney Daily Telegraph *considered the suppression by the Censor, Arthur Calwell, of an edition of the* Sun, *another Sydney newspaper, to be an act of 'monstrous political censorship' and decided to print their objections on Sunday 16 April 1944. Commonwealth security officers served an order on the Editor empowering them to seize all copies. In protest, as can be seen above, later editions of the* Daily Telegraph *appeared with two blank columns where the objections were to appear.*

demand that reports on censorship be submitted to the censor. One paper printed Calwell's comments on the front page, and left a blank space where the paper would have printed its response. Neither side backed down and eventually a High Court decision found in favour of the newspapers. The Government had to relax its regulations.

Restrictions on Political and Religious Rights

Another form of censorship that occurred was the Government's restriction of some political parties and publications.

In June 1940 Menzies banned the Communist Party and several Fascist parties in Australia. The Communist Party was seen as disloyal and the cause of many strikes. In 1939 it was anti-war. However, when Communist Russia was invaded by Germany in 1941 the Communist Party supported Australia's involvement in the war. In December 1941 the ban on the Communist Party was lifted. Between 1939 and 1945 membership of the Party had increased by over 400 per cent.

Other political groups that were banned were those such as the Australia First Movement. It was banned in 1942 as it was sympathetic to Fascism and the Japanese and believed Australia should have a neutral role in the war.

Many foreign publications were banned as well, such as the Russian newspaper *Pravda*, German magazines from the USA and some English and American workers' magazines (Communist sympathisers). The Communist Party traditionally supported workers. After 1942, Japanese magazines were banned as well.

The religious group, the Jehovah's Witnesses, was also banned for publicising anti-war sentiments. Its male members refused to be conscripted and so were interned or sent to work in war industries.

Aliens and Prisoners of War

People whose nationality was the same as that of the enemy (eg German, Italian or Japanese) were called aliens. As early as 4 September 1939, aliens were interned (placed in camps) in Australia. This was one of the Government's first actions under the *National Security Act.* Aliens were considered a danger to national security. Australia in 1939 was still quite racist and these foreigners made the public uneasy. This attitude was not helped by government propaganda inciting hatred of the enemy and warning of enemy spies. However, it was not as bad as the hysteria about foreigners (particularly Germans) of the First World War.

During 1939 and 1940 the Menzies Government interned thousands of Germans and Italians. In 1942 the Curtin Government began interning most of the Japanese civilians.

Early in the war the British Government rounded up thousands of foreign nationals resident in England who had arrived from enemy countries before the outbreak of war. Public panic about the 'enemy within' resulted in Australia and Canada agreeing to take these people and a shipload arrived in Australia on HMT Dunera in 1940. It turned out that the vast majority of these people were strongly anti-Nazi and two-thirds were Jews who had escaped persecution in Germany. The Dunera which transported Australian soldiers to the Middle East in early 1940, brought internees from Britain to Australia later the same year and in 1942 carried reinforcement troops to Batavia. (Australian War Memorial Negative Number 303219)

Interned Italians. A funeral at the 9th Australian Prisoner of War and Internment Camp, Loveday Group, near Barmera, South Australia. Pall bearers lowering the coffin into the grave during the funeral of S13037 Francesco Marco Turra, an Italian internee who died in the camp. (Australian War Memorial Negative Number 064801)

Many were eventually set free when it was realised that they weren't a threat, but restrictions were placed on them. They were made to:

1. Register with authorities
2. Supply photographs of themselves
3. Promise not to act against the British Empire
4. Ask permission before travelling.

Some aliens were attacked and many Australians with foreign-sounding names changed them.

In 1940, 2 500 German and Austrian Jewish refugees from England were brought to Australia on the ship *Dunera*. On the overcrowded *Dunera* the refugees were treated harshly and with much suspicion. On arrival in Australia they were interned at a camp in Hay, New South Wales for months, although their treatment improved once it was acknowledged that they were refugees, not the enemy. Many of the *Dunera* refugees became prominent and influential Australian citizens.

Japanese internees were sent to the Tatura camp in Victoria. Here they ran a clothing factory, made shoes and gardened.

Prisoners of war from Japan, Germany and Italy were also imprisoned in Australian camps. The infamous Cowra Breakout occurred at one such camp in August 1944 when around 1 100 Japanese prisoners of war attempted to escape.

The Cowra Breakout, 5 August 1944

On Saturday 5 August 1944, Japanese prisoners at Cowra staged a breakout that resulted in the deaths of four Australians and 231 Japanese.

The Japanese prisoners of war were dispirited. They'd been captured, which brought great shame upon Japanese soldiers. The war had turned against Japan and some of the prisoners' friends were about to be moved. Human nature is such that friendships develop among prisoners and resentment to the movement and coming separation was rife—the scene was set. Early on 5 August hundreds of Japanese stormed the fences of the camp. Others set fires, some who were immobile committed suicide. Non-participants were murdered.

Hundreds of prisoners escaped and took off into the countryside. In the days that followed 334 prisoners were retaken, of which twenty-five were dead. Eleven of these had committed suicide and two had been hit by trains.

231 Japanese prisoners of war were killed and 108 wounded. The rest were eventually recaptured. Four Australian officers died.

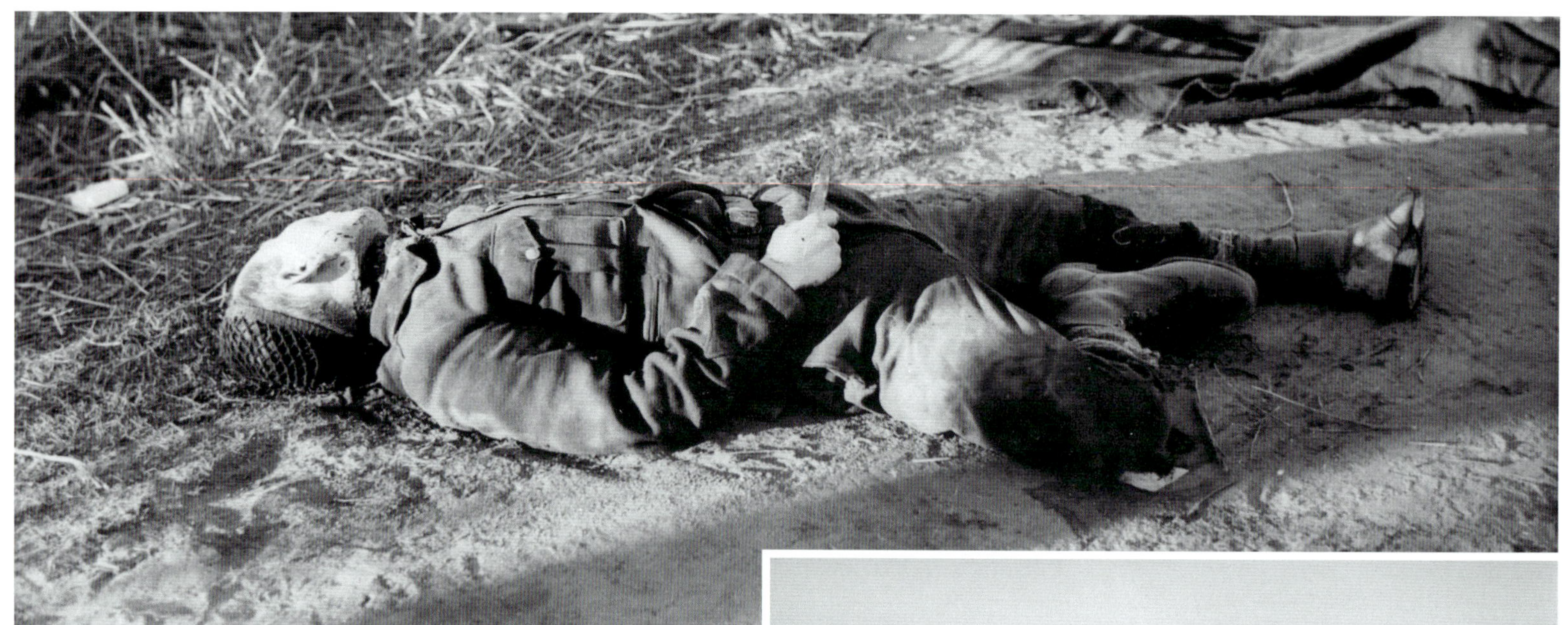

Above: *The dead body of a Japanese prisoner of war who ended his life during the Cowra mass escape in August 1944.* (Australian War Memorial Negative Number 044171)

Right: *Huts destroyed by fire lit by prisoners in the Japanese section of the Cowra prisoner of war camp.* (Australian War Memorial Negative Number 073484)

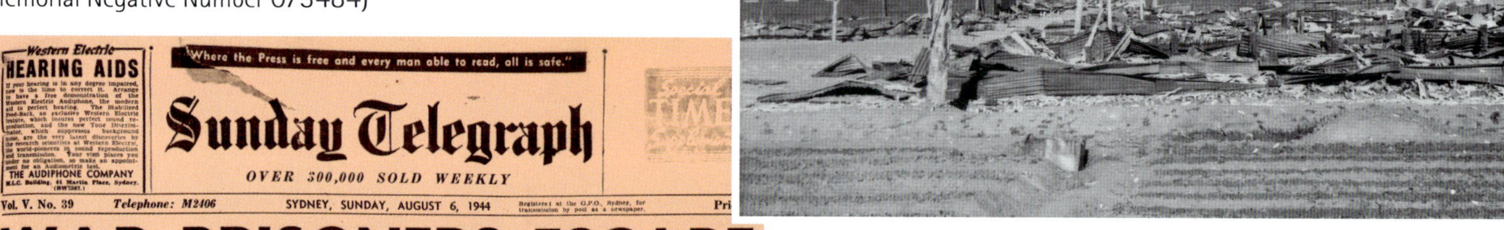

"Where the Press is free and every man able to read, all is safe."

Sunday Telegraph

OVER 300,000 SOLD WEEKLY

Vol. V. No. 39 Telephone: M2406 SYDNEY, SUNDAY, AUGUST 6, 1944

WAR PRISONERS ESCAPE FROM CAMP

Wide search by troops, police

From Our Special Representative

Armed soldiers and civilian police are scouring the Cowra district for prisoners of war who escaped yesterday morning.

The men broke away from the prisoner-of-war camp near Cowra at 2 a.m.

Residents in homesteads and isolated districts have been warned to keep their children and womenfolk indoors at night.

Some prisoners have been recaptured by police and soldiers.

By nightfall others were reported to have reached points 10 to 15 miles from Cowra.

They were moving in different directions.

People living in and near Cowra were warned yesterday in a special broadcast that the escapees might attempt to secure assistance.

They were told to inform military or police authorities if they were approached by escapees, and to keep a sharp watch for strangers.

The number of prisoners who escaped from the camp or their nationality has not been announced.

"We approached cautiously, but found the prisoners quite mild.

"After we had captured them we found they were armed with knives.

Constables McGovern and Cooper also recaptured another escapee during the day.

Tonight I spoke to Mrs. Walter Weir, who "entertained" three of the escaped prisoners at morning tea.

Mrs. Weir lives beside her sister-in-law, Mrs. Robert Weir, at Homewood, six miles out of Cowra.

Mrs. Weir said that three prisoners had apparently slept in the woolshed during the night and emerged soon after breakfast.

"They came up to the house about 9.30," she said.

thanked us and returned to the woolshed also.

"Soon afterwards military police arrived and took the prisoners in charge."

Prime Minister Curtin, who is in Melbourne, and Army Minister Forde, who is in Queensland, were immediately informed of the escapes.

Before full particulars of escapes of prisoners of war can be published, an official Governmental report must be made to the enemy country concerned.

This report, under international agreement, is made through the consular representative of the protecting Power.

Well-behaved

Guards On Roads

New Zealand Escape

ALLIED ARMIES PUSH ON

Allies move s[…] on French po[…]

SUNDAY TELEGRAPH SERVICE A[…]

LONDON, Sat.—American fo[…] south in France are expected […] Nazaire and cut off the whole B[…] sula by tomorrow.

U.S. spearheads today advanced […] hours to Pipriac and Derval.

They are now only 30 miles from […]

Their advance threatens to cut off thousands of German troops in the tip of the peninsula.

Capture of the peninsula will give the Allies the great ports at Brest, Lorient, and St. Malo, as well as those at St. Nazaire and Nantes.

Already the B.B.C. reports fighting in St. Malo.

The Germans are throwing in Tiger tanks in an attempt to prevent the Americans reaching the port.

Nazis Pack Roads

STARVING PARISIANS LIVE ON CARROTS

From DAVID McNICOLL

LONDON, Sat.—Tens of thousands of people in Paris are living on carrots because there is practically no other food, refugees from the capital state.

Nazis murder, loot in Normandy, p. 3, cols. 1, 2.

Left: *A Sydney newspaper front page announcing the Cowra breakout.*

Above: *Following the break-out these knives were recovered in and around the area.* (Australian War Memorial Negative Number 073486)

Conscription

Up until the Second World War Australia didn't have conscription. In the First World War the issue of conscription split not only the Labor Party but the nation. This did not happen when the issue of conscription was brought up in the Second World War. This time, Australia was directly threatened by an aggressive enemy and the population united to defend the country at all costs.

When war broke out in 1939 Australia was not well prepared. The permanent Army numbered about 3 500 and the Citizen Military Force (CMF) or militia was a part-time Army of 80 000 men who could not serve outside Australia. The CMF was available only for home defence.

Prime Minister Menzies called for volunteers and created the Second Australian Imperial Force which headed to Europe and the Middle East in January 1940.

In October 1939 compulsory military training was introduced for the CMF. Single men of 21 years of age were required to complete three months of military training. By mid-1942 all men between 18 and 35 and all single men between 35 and 45, were required to complete military service.

The entry of the Japanese into the war in 1941 brought a new threat to Australia. Curtin and the Labor Government were traditionally against conscription. In fact, Curtin had served jail time in 1916 for his anti-conscription activities. During 1942, however, Australia was in grave danger and it was obvious that the Second AIF could not provide sufficient troops to assist the Americans in their battles against the Japanese. By this time United States troops had arrived to help with Australia's defence and many of them were conscripts. Curtin persuaded the Party to alter the definition of 'Australia' for the purpose of conscription and extend the borders to include New Guinea and the south west Pacific area. The law was passed in February 1943 and the CMF could now be conscripted to defend Australia on foreign soil.

By mid-1943 all available men aged 18-40 who were eligible were in military service.

The Effect of the War on the Australian Economy

Many of the new powers given to the Government in wartime were to have a huge impact on Australia's economy. The Government's new dominance allowed it to control and regulate almost all aspects of the economy so that Australia was properly geared for war.

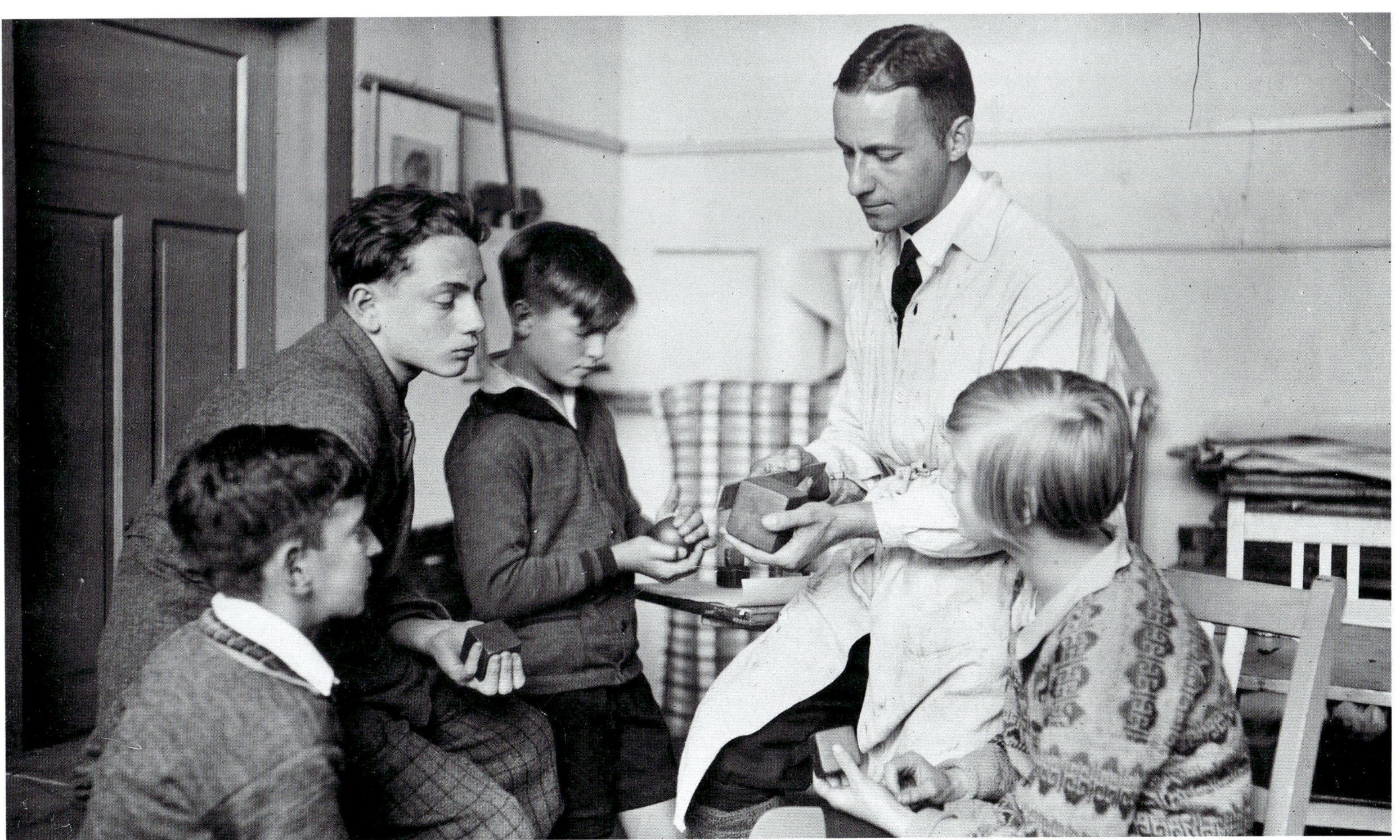

Pictured is one of the Dunera deportees, a distinguished German artist, Ludwig Hirschfield Mack who had won an Iron Cross fighting for Germany in the First World War. But because of his Jewish background he was forced to leave Germany in 1936 and settle in London. He became a teacher and spent the rest of his life in Australia. (Australian War Memorial Negative Number P04558.002)

Key Points:

Political Changes

- The Federal Government's importance and prestige increased.
- Government control over almost every aspect of Australians' lives increased.
- Unions became very concerned about workers' conditions. There were strikes.
- In March 1942 the National Security Act was amended so strikers could be called up.

Many decisions made by employers were now made by the government and employees were under government control.

Wide taxes were introduced to pay for the war. The Federal Treasurer took over the States' power of taxing incomes.

Internment camps were set up for aliens and prisoners of war.

Rationing

The rationing of some goods was needed due to shortages that were occurring. Goods became scarce due to the interruption of supplies from overseas—either because they were directed to the armed forces or because the industry that produced the goods now had to make more essential products for the war effort. Some essential foodstuffs were sent to Great Britain as their food shortages were more severe. As well, the arrival of United States troops in Australia in 1942 impacted on the introduction of rationing as the available food had to be stretched to feed the enormous influx of men. Rationing also ensured equality of sacrifice amongst the population.

Petrol was the first commodity to be rationed. Privately owned cars were allowed to travel about 5 000 km each year. These restrictions were tightened considerably in July 1941 when the allowed travel dropped to 1 500 kilometres and coupons were introduced for the purchase of petrol based on the vehicle's engine capacity.

In 1942, rationing was extended to cover goods such as clothing, tea and sugar. The Rationing Commission controlled rationing. In mid-June, 1942 ration books were introduced. Coupons from the ration books along with money were used to purchase goods.

A service was held in the Melbourne Town Hall on 7 June 1944 to pray for Divine Assistance during the Allied invasion of Europe. Many Church services of this kind were held during the war. (Australian War Memorial Negative Number 141276)

Rationing of Clothing in the Second World War

In the face of rationing, people were encouraged to substitute and make do.

- Women's magazines published tips and recipes on how to achieve this.
- Women were told to paint their legs, or at least draw a back line down the back of their legs, in the place of stockings. Nylon stockings were relatively new and were not sheer as they are today. A straight material join line ran down the back of the leg from top to heel—hence the drawn line to simulate a stocking.
- Men wore 'victory suits'—suits with no lapels or collars and single-breasted.
- Charcoal burners were attached to the backs of cars, the gas from which powered the engine.

Substitutions Encouraged for the Cause of Austerity:

- Petrol—charcoal, household gas.
- Alcohol—home brewed beer, home distilleries for spirits.
- Tea-tea tree, maidenhair fern, red clover blossom, lucerne, chicory essence.
- Tobacco-musk leaves, cured gum leaves.
- Clothing-flour bags.

In 1942 the Minister for War Organisation of Industry, Mr Dedman, attempted to 'kill' Christmas! A ban was placed on advertising related to Christmas, New Year or Easter. Dedman even suggested gift giving be prohibited. It was deemed inappropriate that there should be excessive spending on luxuries and wasting of resources in a time of sacrifice.

Butter rationing was introduced in 1943 to alleviate a shortage in Britain. As well, a speed limit of 60km/ph was imposed, supposedly to save rubber. The rationing of clothes was expanded to include curtains and sheets. There were other restrictions on clothing, such as the banning of mutton sleeves (a wide-style of sleeve) so as not to waste fabric.

Meat rationing began in January 1944. Each person was limited to about 1kg meat weekly. A very complicated coupon system existed depending on the type or cut of meat you wished to have. Sausages, offal, rabbit and chicken were not rationed.

At different times throughout the war, eggs and milk were rationed when shortages arose. Other goods were banned

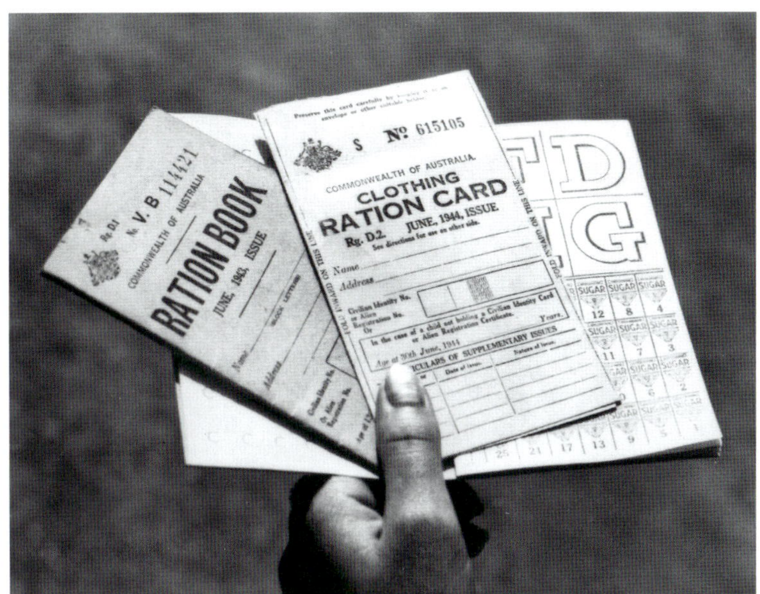

Ration cards which were needed in order to purchase food and clothing. (Australian War Memorial Negative Number 042770)

from being produced altogether, such as hats, jewellery, swimsuits, toys, lawnmowers and children's party dresses.

Reductions were ordered in the production of beer and spirits. Hotel trading hours were shortened in an effort to reduce spending on alcohol.

Ration Coupons

Coupons were not just exchanged between customer and retailer. They were used throughout the chain of supply, right through to the producers.

A black market soon developed and there were few Australians who didn't buy things on the black market at one time or another. Luxury items were the most sought after, as

A fund-raising clothing stall for the Australian Comfort Fund at a Carnival held in Martin Place, Sydney. No ration coupons were necessary so the stall was busy. (Australian War Memorial Negative Number 108042)

A Melbourne city store enquiry section set up to give customers information about rationing and coupons for food and clothing. (Australian War Memorial Negative Number 136413)

well as alcohol. In September 1942 the 'Black Marketing Act' was passed to address the problem. Fines began at £1000.

A lasting impact of rationing was its effect on Australian's health, which improved. Obesity levels fell. Children received healthier food and the population as a whole became more health conscious.

A Time Line of Rationed Goods

Item	Introduced	Concluded
Petrol	July 1940	1950
Tea	March 1942	July 1950
Clothing	May 1942	June 1948
Sugar	August 1942	July 1947
Butter	June 1943	June 1950
Meat	January 1944	June 1948

Manpower Regulations

A beneficial effect of war on an economy is that unemployment often disappears. The unemployed can take over the jobs of men who leave to fight and changes in the economy brought about by the need for munitions and/or self sufficiency can create more jobs.

This is what happened in Australia. Unfortunately, the workforce wasn't large enough to accommodate the needs of a war economy. Thousands of women joined the workforce and their role will be discussed in the section on women's roles in the war. More regulation was needed to manage the available workforce. Those who worked in so-called 'reserved occupations' (jobs considered vital to the war effort) could not change jobs or leave to join the military. Nevertheless, there was still a shortfall of workers.

A Directorate of Manpower was set up in 1942 to address this problem. New regulations were added to the National Security Act. Curtin announced new controls over wages, prices and profits to make sure everyone was making an equal 'sacrifice' for the war effort. The 'equality of sacrifice' had been a major complaint during the First World War. In March 1942 all adult civilians were issued identity cards. Unfortunately, 1942 was a critical year in Australia's defence and the size of the armed forces expanded, with the result that fewer workers existed. Those in non-essential jobs were expected to either join the military or move to an 'essential job'. By the end of 1942 more than 400 000 people had been moved to essential jobs.

Many disgruntled workers began to shirk their responsibilities and earned the wrath of the officials of the manpower commission. For example:

- In an unprecedented step, New Year's Day 1943 was declared a normal working day. In Sydney, around 200 people were prosecuted for absenteeism on that day. More than 30 000 workers in New South Wales took the day off!
- Snap raids by manpower authorities occurred in places like pubs, sporting events, cinemas and restaurants. It was illegal to be an absentee.

Manpower Shortages were Most Acute in Transport, Housing and the Public Service.

Towards the end of 1943 the size of the Army began to be reduced, easing the pressure on the available workforce somewhat.

The Manpower regulations were not welcomed by all. There was a great deal of resentment. Some people suffered a drop in wages. Some felt that men in essential jobs were avoiding having to join the armed forces. Many businesses failed. Others simply resented yet another government intrusion in their lives.

Industry

Primary Industry (Agriculture)

Australia's farmers did quite well during the war, although agriculture as a whole declined. During the Depression of the 1930s many men left the land for manufacturing jobs or the armed services. Japanese expansion into the islands of the South Pacific meant that fertiliser could not be obtained. Added to this was a drought in 1944.

On the positive side, Britain continued to purchase many raw materials from Australia, although the war restricted shipping the products. In 1939 Britain agreed to buy Australia's surplus wool clip throughout the war at a good price. Wheat purchased by Britain needed to be stored awaiting shipment because there were very few ships available to transport it. The market for Australian goods also increased with the arrival of United States troops in Australia. However, farmers had to diversify their crops because of American demand for tomatoes, vegetables and fruit. The US Army and Red Cross ran farms specifically to cultivate such produce for the Americans.

Secondary Industry (Manufacturing)

Traditionally, Australia exported primary products and imported manufactured goods. The war had a huge effect on the manufacturing sector of Australia's economy for several reasons:

- Some of the countries Australia imported manufactured goods from were now the enemy
- Shipping was not available for merchant purposes or was severely interrupted
- Australia began producing war materials

In 1914–18 the impact of war on Australia's economy resulted in severe shortages of essential items. As a result of this the inter-war years had seen a continued growth in the country's manufacturing sector. Nevertheless, there was still a further and significant expansion in industries such as chemicals, tools, steel, shipbuilding and medical equipment as the Second World War progressed. In terms of war materials, Australia produced weapons and even aircraft. These products will be discussed further below.

The Wacket Trainer, designed and built in Australia was a staple training aircraft with the Royal Australian Air Force and was used throughout the war. Here men and women employed by the Commonwealth Aircraft Corporation are busily assembling the aeroplane for service. (Australian War Memorial Negative Number 011598/25)

A poster displayed and issued in about 1943 advertising training for men in the war effort. (Australian War Memorial Negative Number ARTV01083)

Munitions

In 1940 a Directorate of Munitions was created by Prime Minister Menzies. The Director-General of Munitions, Essington Lewis, was a BHP director and BHP's plants had been gearing up for war for some time.

By the beginning of 1942, heavy industry was manufacturing war materials such as textiles, ammunition, small arms, chemicals, anti-aircraft guns, tanks and radios. Hundreds of aircraft were being built. By the middle of 1943 munitions manufacture had reached its peak, employing over 100 000 workers. In 1944 the numbers of workers in munitions factories began to reduce dramatically.

Industrial Action

The war created full employment for workers, and even though prices were regulated by the Government, taxation increased. Most workers were not better off. However, the unions tried to co-operate with the Government to assist the war effort. Any strikes were usually localised and short.

There were industrial disputes but not to the same extent as those of the First World War era. The most serious strikes (accounting for over 80% of all disputes) were amongst the coalminers who regularly felt they were treated unfairly.

Women busy at work in the small arms munitions factory at Footscray, Victoria in 1939. (Australian War Memorial Negative Number 000007/22)

Manufacturing steel for the munitions industry at Port Kembla, New South Wales. (Australian War Memorial Negative Number 012658)

Hoeing pineapples with a rotary hoe at an Army farm in the Northern Territory. Fresh fruit, vegetables, eggs and poultry were supplied to troops and hospitals from eight army farms in the district.
(Australian War Memorial Negative Number 014723)

There were significant strikes in 1940 and 1941 and a six-month strike in 1944. In 1942 a regulation was passed allowing the Government to call up strikers for military or labour service.

Absenteeism was high in some industries, particularly amongst workers who'd been forced (under manpower regulations) into unpleasant or what were considered to be boring and repetitive work.

Taxation

The Federal Government's increase in power in the Second World War was most significant in the area of taxation. The war was expensive and new taxes were introduced to cover the cost.

The Federal Government took over control of income tax from the states in May 1942 under the Uniform Taxation Act. As well, the tax-free threshold was lowered (those with lower incomes were now taxed), which more than doubled the number of taxpayers. In 1944 the rate of income tax was increased as nearly half of the Government's income went towards war costs.

In 1945 a new Social Service Contribution Tax was levied to pay for the social service plans introduced during the war (such as child endowment, widows' pensions etc) as well as the various social services that would be required after the war for ex-servicemen.

To provide fresh meat for soldiers in the North West area of Australia, the Army established its own abbatoirs about 16 kilometres north of Katherine. (Australian War Memorial Negative Number 014294)

Banking

In November 1941 the Government introduced the Wartime Banking Control Regulations. This meant that the Government could control the lending policies and interest rates and monitor foreign exchange actions. Banks were forced to maintain a Commonwealth Bank account so that the Government could control the amount of money in circulation.

Army personnel working on the wharves during a strike by wharf labourers. (Australian War Memorial Negative Number 050650)

Soldiers guiding a sling of merchandise in the ship loading process. (Australian War Memorial Negative Number 050655)

Urgently needed cargo being unloaded by Army and Air Force personnel during a strike. (Australian War Memorial Negative Number 050662)

Key Points:

Economic Changes

- Rationing introduced.
- Production of many goods—particularly 'luxury' items—banned.
- Directorate of Manpower controlled workers.
- The war promoted industrial and technological change.
- Munitions industry established in Australia.
- The economy was restructured towards manufacturing.
- The value of industrial production increased 100% between 1937-1945.
- Increase in chemical, rubber, metal goods and car industries.
- Australian science and research fields found to be lacking.

The Effect of War on Australian Society

The increase in the Government's power had a huge effect on people's everyday lives and on society as a whole. The population's civil liberties were greatly reduced and this caused much resentment. Even so, Australians generally accepted the restrictions placed upon them due to the seriousness of the war and the fact that this time the front line was on Australia's doorstep. 'Austerity' was the key and people were prepared to do their bit for the war effort.

Blackouts, Air Raid Drills and Sandbags

Blackouts began in 1941. Air raid precautions were also introduced as it seemed increasingly likely Japan would enter the war. To prevent Japanese landings, barbed wire and concrete obstructions were placed on the beaches and weapons installations were built.

Blackouts and brownouts were enforced so that cities and towns could not be identified from the air. The amount of light required at night was restricted—houselights, street lights, headlights. Towns and cities near the coast were affected by these. In Melbourne there were no street lights, but in Sydney half the streetlights were on. If driving at night, a car's headlights had to be covered allowing minimal light on the road. However, this created fatalities in traffic

Above: *A Royal Australian Air Force corporal waits at a tram stop to escort members of the Womens Auxiliary Australian Air Force back to their camp during a blackout.* (Australian War Memorial Negative Number 137595)

Below: *With no street lighting at night, the many roads without footpaths were particularly hazardous. A poster issued by the National Safety Council of Australia for the State Emergency Services, Victoria.* (Australian War Memorial Negative Number ARTV03272)

Above: *Grim warnings. In case of an air raid—an illustration of what NOT to do. The correct procedure was: lights off, stay inside and take cover. The poster was issued by the National Safety Council of Australia for the State Emergency Services, Victoria.* (Australian War Memorial Negative Number ARTV03271)

and people were asked to wear bright clothing to make them more visible to drivers.

In 1942, as the war moved closer to Australia, air raid drills and sirens were introduced. These were practised in schools, businesses and streets. Public transport was camouflaged. Sandbags were used around buildings and windows were covered by boards or taped up in case of bomb strikes or as protection from flying debris. Flags were removed from government buildings as they were likely targets.

People built air raid shelters and trenches in their homes and public shelters were built by the Government. Street signs were removed.

There were planned and actual evacuations. Thousands of people moved voluntarily from the coast (where the threat was seen as greatest) to inland regions.

Rural Society

Those living in the country areas of Australia suffered more

The night appearance of Melbourne city during the brownout, *an easing of lighting restrictions.* (Australian War Memorial Negative Number 139182)

than those in the cities. Drought in 1940 and 1944 only made things worse. Some of the people in non essential businesses moved from country towns to take up occupations in the city

Farmers had longer distances to travel than city-dwellers but the petrol rationing and restrictions on distances travelled were the same as their city counterparts. Tourism was affected for the same reason—people could not travel out to the country.

Another major problem was the effect of the war on the workforce. Many young people left the country towns to join the armed forces or take jobs in the cities. Women, refugees, interned aliens and trustworthy prisoners of war were used as farm labour.

Leisure Activities

Many leisure activities were curtailed during the war years. The sale of beer and spirits was restricted. Gambling was discouraged and the first Saturday of the month became race-free. Nevertheless, the 1940 Melbourne Cup attracted huge crowds and record gambling figures. In 1943 the ban on race meetings was lifted.

Sporting activities were restricted for two main reasons:

1. It was seen as frivolous given it was a time of war.
2. Men fit enough to play sport should be in the armed services and fighting for the country.

As a result many sporting matches were cancelled.

United States Troops in Australia

Australia was a logical base for United States troops involved in the war in the Pacific. United States troops began arriving in Australia 'secretly' shortly after the Japanese attack on Pearl Harbour. The media were not allowed to announce their arrival. In March 1942 the arrival of the United States troops was made public. Hundreds of thousands of American troops would eventually arrive in Australia.

At first the Americans were welcomed, but, later in the war, as the Japanese threat began to wane, many Australians began to focus on the negative aspects of their presence. However, it must be remembered that the Americans were only based in some cities and the majority of Australians would never have had any contact with them at all. But as it happened, these troops were certainly the largest

The American transport Chaumont *which brought United States troops to Australia as part of the Pensacola Convoy in 1941 and 1942.* (Australian War Memorial Negative Number 303095)

United States Army troops queue for a meal, probably of vegetables and soup. (Australian War Memorial Negative Number 150068)

single entry of people to Australia in our history at the time.

Australian men felt threatened by the American soldiers because they were well-paid. Many young women were attracted to them for the same reason, but women who showed any affection for American soldiers were often criticised and accused of having 'low morals'. The Australian men believed their girlfriends were being stolen from them.

The American soldiers could afford to buy luxurious goods for women and themselves while Australia was in the grip of the wartime austerity drive. An Australian Army private received about half the pay of a United States private. The spending power of the United States troops pushed up prices, boosted the black market trade and ensured they always got the best service. This caused more resentment.

In return, many United States soldiers resented the Australian servicemen stationed on the homefront. The Americans were conscripts on leave from the fighting and saw themselves as being in the region to defend and perhaps die for Australia, a foreign country, while Australian servicemen and civilians in the street were enjoying life at home. It was a serious misunderstanding.

Resentment towards the American troops sometimes flared into violence, but it often went unreported in the press for fear of negatively affecting morale. The 'battle of Brisbane' of 26 November 1942 (United States Thanksgiving)

United States troops from an anti-aircraft unit marching from 'United States of America Transport Docks' on arrival at an Australian port. (Australian War Memorial Negative Number P02018.066)

A United States serviceman being given some Australian hospitality. Countless Australians threw open their doors to provide comforts for the young men far from home, who would be fighting for the protection of Australia. (Australian War Memorial Negative Number 012176)

American swing music was at the height of its popularity during the Second World War and had a huge influence on Australian musicians. This popular band of serving Australian soldiers are members of the 36th Battalion, Australian Military Forces, performing in Jacquinot Bay, New Britain in 1945. (Australian War Memorial Negative Number P02217.005)

Black American servicemen were not able to fraternise with white troops at clubs or dances—this club was for the use of Afro-American troops only. The United States 5th Air Corps Orchestra is playing and the two dancers are from New York. (Australian War Memorial Negative Number 015578)

was the most notorious incident and was not mentioned by the media. In this incident, thousands of drunken Australians had congregated around a United States Army canteen. United States troops fired some shots in an attempt to disperse the crowd, but one Australian was killed and others wounded. A riot quickly spread through Brisbane.

There were also a number of murders and assaults carried out by United States servicemen, such as the 'brownout murderer' Private Edward Leonski, who was eventually hanged in a Melbourne Prison. Murder was a capital offence in Australia at that time.

Tension was also created between the Americans and Australians based on race. There were two reasons for this:

1. Some Australians disliked having black American troops in their community. Australia was a very 'closed community' at that time because of its isolation. Discrimination towards the Aboriginal people was practised by the Government and by the majority of citizens. Hence, as Afro-Americans had black skin, they were seen as second class citizens by many Australians.
2. On the other hand, there were others, more enlightened in the community who disapproved of the inferior way black American troops were treated. (It is important to remember that segregation was still practised in parts of the United States). For instance, this was the time when jazz and swing music was hugely popular among young people and white American service musicians often joined Australian bands at Cabarets. However, black American servicemen and musicians were excluded from performing or from taking part in the dancing and had to listen outside the doors of the venues. Some enlightened young Australians joined the black servicemen outside and danced with them there.

   The arrival of the Americans had a significant effect on Australians' diets. The US soldiers ate food that Australians did not. The Australian diet was meat, vegetables and beer. The Americans drank coffee and orange juice. They ate pork and avocados, though they *did* drink beer, but were used to a lower alcohol content. The typical American hamburger and cola drinks were demanded and hamburger cafes soon sprang up in cities.

During 1944 the American troops were withdrawn, with almost all of them having left by October. Despite the negative image of women who associated with American troops, almost 12 000 marriages occurred, many of which unfortunately ended in divorce. Some women were very naive about the life they were going to lead, while others were abandoned. On the other hand there were many very successful marriages, and Australian 'war brides' still live with their families in the United States today.

Key Points:

Social Changes

- Austerity was the key word.
- Gambling—racing—sports were discouraged and often restricted or banned.
- Women were not to wear makeup or silk stockings.
- Travel restrictions were in place.
- Air raid shelters, trenches were constructed. Air raid drills became normal practice.
- Blackouts and brownouts occurred.
- The public were warned about idle talk for fear of spies.
- Propaganda was used to enforce regulations, boost morale and encourage enlistment.
- Buildings were sandbagged.
- Weapons installations were built on the coast.

Adelaide River, Northern Territory. Two signalwomen write letters and do fancy work in front of their hut 'Cupid's Corner' at the 69th Australian Women's Army Barracks. (Australian War Memorial Negative Number 069159)

The Role of Women on the Australian Home Front

After the First World War, the women who had stepped into men's roles or entered the workforce went back to their traditional roles as wives and mothers. The number of women in the workforce altered little as a result of the First World War.

In the Second World War, women played a much greater role as they were not prepared to sit back and simply knit socks and mittens. Society assumed that this is what they would do, as they had households to run and mouths to feed. As the threat to Australia intensified, many women wanted to play a more significant part in the war effort.

There were three main areas where women could become involved in the war effort:

1. Serving in the armed forces. The only women who were at the Front were nurses and some other women (mostly still in medical roles). Most women worked in other positions in the armed forces on the home front.
2. Working in industry.
3. Joining voluntary organisations.

At first the Government was reluctant to allow women to take on roles outside their traditional ones in the home. However, as the Japanese threat increased and manpower shortages became more critical, women were allowed to take a more active part in the war effort—but still not to the same extent (or for the same financial rewards) as men.

Women in the Armed Forces

Women joined the armed forces for a number of reasons. Some felt that at last they could be actively involved in the war effort. Others had fathers, brothers or husbands in the services so also wanted to join.

The women's armed forces organisations were formed to free up men for combat roles. Women were paid at about two-thirds of the male rate.

In early 1941 the Royal Australian Air Force (RAAF) was allowed to establish the Women's Auxiliary Australian Air Force (WAAAF). This change came about because of a severe shortage of wireless telegraphists. Some women who enlisted had taken the initiative by already training themselves. The WAAAF was the first and largest women's armed services group.

At its peak there were over 18 000 women in the WAAAF. They performed jobs such as electricians, flight mechanics and meteorological assistants, as well as having roles in the fields of transport, catering and signals.

Over 700 women held a commissioned rank but were paid much less than their male counterparts.

From 1941 to 1947 about 27 000 women served in the WAAAF. 57 died in service.

The Australian Women's Army Service (AWAS) was established in August 1941. By the end of the war over 20 000 women had enlisted in the service. In the following years they served as typists, wireless mechanics, drivers, instrument operators, orderlies, stewardesses, signalwomen and stenographers. Over 3 000 women manned the Fixed Defences of Australia as part of the Royal Australian Artillery. In the later years of the war, the War Cabinet gave some AWAS personnel special permission to serve overseas.

The Women's Royal Australian Naval Service (WRANS) began as 14 female wireless telegraphists in April 1941. In 1943 the number increased to 1 000 but throughout the remainder of the war the numbers of WRANS did not exceed 3 000. Their jobs were generally the same as those in the AWAS. Many held positions where they had to be secretive about the nature of their work, such as in ciphers.

Left: *This poster demonstrates the attitude to women of that time—women attend to the clothing and home needs, while men operate the machines and fight in the jungle. In the bottom left corner is the warning 'Don't talk, idle gossip may sink a clothing ship'.*
(Australian War Memorial Negative Number ARTV01064)

Below: *Australian Women's Land Army members in the field harvesting large crops of tomatoes which are to be canned for the troops.* (Australian War Memorial Negative Number 014929)

An Australian Women's Land Army camp in Biloela, Queensland, 1943–1945. Posing in front of the buildings is Grace Taylor, who was an artist in civilian life and painted the cartoons on the hut walls. (Australian War Memorial Negative Number P01624.008)

The Women's Australian National Service (WANS) marching in Martin Place, Sydney, probably in a War Bonds parade of the combined voluntary women's services groups. The gauntlets (long gloves) indicate that the wearers are drivers or riders. (Australian War Memorial Negative Number P03099.002)

Nora Heyson. Transport Driver (Aircraftwoman Florence Miles), May 1945, *oil on canvas, Cairns, Australia, 66.6 x 81.8 cm.* (ART24393). *Nora Heyson saw Florence as a 'young, forward lass', who had enlisted in the Womens Auxiliary Australian Air Force in 1942, aged 21. This is a compelling portrait of a confident young woman who, despite the masculine uniform and large leather gloves, retains her femininity.*

The peak of women's involvement in these armed services was in 1944, when approximately 40 000 women were serving.

Women in Industry

The employment of women in industry was a significant social effect of the Second World War. By mid-1943, about 145 000 were employed in war production.

In 1941, Menzies altered the list of reserved occupations, freeing up more men to fight. Women were to fill their vacant positions. It was soon clear that women were capable of performing work traditionally done by men; however, they were paid only little more than half the rate of men. By 1942 steps had been taken to equalise (to an extent) pay rates, but even so women were never paid exactly the same as men in the same job.

After Singapore fell in February 1942 there was a significant increase in the number of women employed in industry. Australia was suffering chronic manpower shortages and manpower regulations were bringing many more women into the workforce. All single women who were not in 'useful' employment and who refused to work in the services or an essential job could be conscripted into war work. The work was often monotonous and many women resented having to work. No allowance was made for women with husbands or families who had to work as well as having to maintain a household.

In rural industry, women also took over men's jobs in farms and orchards. The Australian Women's Land Army (AWLA) was created in July 1942. It was a volunteer group and women had to go where they were sent, often to remote

Key Points:

The Role of Women

- Women were encouraged to enter the workforce to replace or free up men for service. They worked in factories and munitions plants.
- Wages were unequal. Women received about 54% of the male wage. Trade unions were unhappy as it made women cheaper to employ than men.
- In 1941, women began to join the armed forces. This was to free up men for active service. Only nurses and a few other special positions could serve overseas. Women joined the WAAAF, AWAS, and WRANS in mostly clerical, transport and signals and communications work.
- Women joined the Women's Land Army to assist on the farms.
- Women also took part in voluntary work—making and sending comforts, letters and fundraising. There were also 'paramilitary' voluntary groups the women got involved in.

A woman testing dial sights, fire control equipment used on 25 pounder gun howitzers. The dial sights were manufactured at a factory which before the war was engaged in the production of watch cases. Australia was the only British dominion manufacturing this particular type of dial sight. (Australian War Memorial Negative Number P00784.154)

regions. Their work was essential to keep up with the high demand for fruit, vegetables, meat and particularly flax.

Women in industry also had to contend with the negative attitudes of men and even other women. There was still a pervading feeling that a woman's place was in the home and the war was 'men's work'. Many conservative and religious groups were outraged at married women entering the workforce. The Unions were concerned for their members who may find their job taken by a lower-paid female worker on their return from service-essential war work. Many did not like the idea of women being financially independent.

Women's Volunteer Organisations

During the First World War, women's voluntary work usually involved knitting for the soldiers, making comfort packs or raising money for the war effort. These kinds of activities occurred during the Second World War but there were also more military-style volunteer groups created. Less-structured volunteer work that women took part in was to look after troops on leave—providing food, housing and entertainment for them.

There were also many volunteer organisations that women joined:

- Australian Comforts Fund: mostly knitting—balaclavas, gloves, jumpers, socks. This group had also operated during the First World War and was re-established in 1940.
- Red Cross: fund-raising, knitting and making comforts for troops, visiting hospitalised troops and providing comforts for them. The Red Cross also provided a free blood transfusion service. By 1944 there were 400 000 members.
- Red Cross Voluntary Aid Detachments (VADs) were trained medical staff (women) who helped out in convalescent hospitals.
- Women's Voluntary National Register.
- Women's Auxiliary of the National Defence League: women and school children in this group made over 150 000 camouflage nets.

Women in some of these organisations also did work such as child care for working mothers.

Of a more militaristic nature were the following women's volunteer organisations. They often had uniforms and learnt skills they felt might be useful in wartime. They also hoped to be recognised by the Government for their efforts.

- Women's Australian National Services (NSW); these women learnt signalling, first aid and ambulance driving. They practised air raid and military drills. This group was designed to be an 'umbrella' group for all the smaller organisations that had sprung up. It was recognised by the State, but not Federal Government and it also failed to reign in the number of paramilitary groups being formed.
- Cavalry Corps
- Women's Auxiliary Service Patriots
- Women's Emergency Signalling Corps
- Women's Army Corps

The Home Front Under Attack!

In 1942 Australian soil was attacked by an enemy for the first time. The two most significant attacks were the air raid on Darwin in February and the later shelling of Sydney by Japanese midget submarines in May. Japanese bombs and shells landed on many Australian coastal towns. Broome suffered the second-worst air raid in March 1942, when approximately 70 were killed. Newcastle was shelled. Most of the (air) bombing raids (97 in total) occurred along Australia's northern coastline, from Port Headland east to Townsville.

The Attack on Darwin, February 1942

The north coast of Australia was bombed around 100 times between 1942 and the end of 1943. The major attack was on Darwin on 19 February 1942, when over 200 were killed. Eight ships had been sunk and another 12 were damaged. 20 aircraft were lost. Many buildings were destroyed.

The Japanese attack on Darwin was prompted by Japan's wish to deter the United States from using the town as a base. There were also merchant ships and war ships moored in Port Darwin. The reaction in Darwin was a debacle.

After the fall of Singapore an invasion was expected in Darwin. In preparation, thousands of civilians had been evacuated inland to Adelaide River. A mass of people using any form of transport they could find headed south.

At 9.55am on 19 February about 200 Japanese planes flew above Darwin. Many mistook them for United States planes. There were no early warning systems and usually the drone of planes or bombs dropping was the first sign of attack. In fact, many were guided by their dogs, as the dogs seemed to sense the impending danger! Once the bombs began dropping, the military garrison in Darwin panicked. Many took off into the bush, some turning up later in Adelaide and Melbourne.

A train was quickly organised to evacuate women and children but men pushed them off the carriages and boarded instead. Drunken military police were sent in to restore order but began firing into the air, causing more chaos. People began ducking for cover when another air raid siren rang out

SS Neptunia explodes as survivors leave the fiercely burning Zealandia *during the air attack on Darwin, Northern Territory on 19 February 1942.* (Australian War Memorial Negative Number 126807)

The 'Priceless ingredient' in . . . Orlando WINES . . . . . . is the reputation of the maker built up over 100 years

Greatest Daily Net Sales of Any Paper in New South Wales

HIGH TIDES: 12.24 a.m. (4ft. 4in.). 12.33 p.m. (4ft. 1in.).

Daily Telegraph AND DAILY NEWS

Vol. VI. No. 287 (New Series) Telephone: M2406 SYDNEY, FRIDAY, FEBRUARY 20, 1942 Registered at the G.P.O., Sydney, for transmission by post as a newspaper. Price, 2d

ARE YOU READY? willing and able to LAUGH OUT LOUD! Then the right spot for you to-day is the STATE THEATRE, when Judy Canova arrives in her new hilarity hit, "PUDDIN' HEAD."

TWO JAPANESE RAIDS ON DARWIN

EDITORIAL

We Will Show That We Can Take It, Too

DARWIN has been bombed.

With our minds still bemused by 150 years of happy security, we find this news of an enemy's first violence almost unbelievable.

But the stark, unpleasant fact remains—Japan, swollen with victory, has opened her offensive against us.

What are we to do?

That question every Australian must answer for himself at once.

He must answer it after a cold and detached assessment of the facts, without tenderness to himself or his own special sectional interests, with only one thing in mind—what is best for Australia?

There are two alternative lines of action.

Let us consider them without baulking at any of the facts.

Australia, invaded, can—ask Japan to make peace or stand up and fight.

In every country there are people who think they can escape the suffering of war by coming to terms with the enemy.

They think that thus they can preserve their lives and some of their possessions.

It is necessary to look squarely at this proposition.

Honorable Loot, Gentlemen!

THE Japanese would probably behave most graciously in offering us escape from the war, for that would solve a lot of their difficulties: they would no longer have to fear an Allied offensive from this part of the world.

They would say: "Gentlemen, we are delighted to help you out of this foolish mess you have got yourselves into.

"Let us now live as good neighbors.

"We want your wheat and wool (And how they want it!).

93 Planes Take Part In Attacks

No Details Of Damage Available Yet: At Least Four Raiders Down

After bombing Darwin at 10.35 (Sydney time) yesterday morning, Japanese planes made a second raid in the afternoon.

These were the first attacks ever to be made on Australian mainland territory.

In the first raid, which lasted an hour, 72 twin-engine bombers, accompanied by an escort of fighters, were over the town.

Twenty-one bombers made the second raid yesterday afternoon.

Four enemy planes were brought down.

Announcing the raids late last night, the Prime Minister said that damage to property was considerable, but reports so far to hand did not give precise particulars of loss of life.

Attacks Most Grave—Curtin

Darwin (1975 air-miles from Canberra to address the special session In addition to the radio communi-

New Jap Offensive In Burma

Daily Telegraph Service and A.A.P.

RANGOON, Thursday.—Japanese forces thrusting into Burma have launched strong attacks against the new British defence line west of the Bilin River (80 miles east of Rangoon).

"A big new battle has begun," the B.B.C. says. "Heavy fighting has spread along the whole Bilin River front."

A British communique says the Japanese crossed the Bilin River on Tuesday in small boats.

"At some places fighting raged all night long, and was continued yesterday morning," the communique adds.

"Our forces are holding their positions and fighting strongly.

"Indian Air Force fighter planes went into action over Burma for the first time as British patrols south-west of the Bilin line clashed with Japanese forces moving up rapidly to attack our new positions.

"The enemy attacked our left flank, resulting in hand-to-hand fighting.

"Gurkhas counter-attacked and restored the situation. R.A.F. and Indian Air Forces reconnoitred."

Rangoon The Prize

London reports say that British bombers, aiding the land troops in the defence of the Bilin River, are hammering Japanese positions.

Japanese claims to be within 30 miles of Rangoon are discounted.

The London Daily Telegraph's correspondent says: "The Battle of Burma has begun in earnest.

"The invaders, despite severe losses,

The front page of the Sydney Daily Telegraph *the day after the Japanese attack on Darwin.*

and the train driver started the train, leaving the women and children of Darwin abandoned.

Looting and vandalism broke out in Darwin. The military threatened to shoot those who tried to stop it. A Royal Commission was set up to investigate the attack on Darwin and reported these events.

The day after the attack, the Government reported 15 dead.

In March 1942 and the months following Darwin was hit again, eventually suffering 64 raids up to November 1943. Simultaneously, merchant vessels were being attacked by the Japanese off the coast of eastern Australia.

The Australian public was deceived about the scale of the Darwin attack for many years, as the Government did not want to create panic or lower the public's morale. It is important to remember that Darwin was very isolated at that time and communications were not like those we enjoy today. The Government later announced seventeen dead. Some historians today regard the official figures released after the War of 243 dead and 400 injured as conservative. Their estimates are closer to 1 000. Darwin had many itinerant workers whose numbers are unknown.

Japanese Submarines in Sydney Harbour, 31 May 1942

Sydney Harbour became a Japanese target because of the warships moored there. Before dawn on 30 May, 1942, an unmarked Japanese seaplane flew into Sydney Harbour on a reconnaissance mission. The plane was mistaken as an American aircraft and ignored.

At about 8pm on 31 May three Japanese midget submarines entered Sydney Harbour while the mother submarine waited out at sea. The midget submarines each carried two men and two torpedoes.

The first submarine became tangled in the anti-submarine net. A lookout noticed the unusual movement in the water and shone a light on the submarine at around 8.30pm. He raised the alarm. At around 10.30pm a Japanese sailor blew up the submarine.

The second submarine's periscope was sighted around Garden Island. This sighting caused absolute panic. Lights, flares and shell explosions lit up the Harbour. Ferry passengers were caught up in the middle of it all.

The USS *Chicago* and HMAS *Whyalla* opened fire at the spot where the periscope was seen. Depth charges were dropped. Then, a third submarine was seen but it somehow

The attack on Sydney Harbour by midget submarines on 31 May 1942. This submarine was rammed and sunk by gunfire before she could fire her torpedoes. (Australian War Memorial Negative Number 060696)

managed to dive out of the way of depth charges.

The submarines fired torpedoes at the Chicago at about 12.30pm. One was a dud, the other missed the ship and exploded against a dock wall. Unfortunately, the force of the blast sank HMAS *Kuttabul*, an old ferry being used as a depot ship with troops aboard, killing 19. The second submarine then disappeared.

The pandemonium continued. The third submarine was sighted in Taylor's Bay. Depth charges were dropped until the submarine was destroyed.

Ferries continued to cross the harbour. Many passengers thought they were witnessing an air raid or a navy drill. Waterfront residents described the searchlights and flares as being like watching fireworks. Houses were shaken and windows broken. Many people panicked and ran out into the streets.

In June, Sydney's eastern suburbs were also shelled. The shells landed in Rose Bay, Woollahra and Bellevue Hill. Many residents fled west to the Blue Mountains and beyond, convinced that a full-scale Japanese attack was imminent. One woman smashed her Japanese dinner set in protest! The shelling in general did little damage. Roads were broken up and windows smashed. One casualty had a broken leg. A block of flats in Rose Bay suffered damage. Several houses had smashed windows and interior and exterior walls from the shells landing in their houses. Injuries to the occupants were relatively minor.

Shortly after the shelling of east Sydney, another Japanese submarine surfaced at Newcastle. Newcastle suburbs were shelled and Fort Scratchley fired back in return. The attack was more severe than at Sydney. Fortunately the shells caused no casualties and only one exploded. One house was sprayed with shrapnel fragments. A second shell fell on a tram stop but failed to explode. Train passengers to Newcastle were sent to air raid shelters.

Australians were no longer complacent about the war.

The Post-War Home Front

In 1944 the strains of war were beginning to tell on the Australian population. It was fairly clear that the Allies would beat Germany and the Japanese were being pushed out of the south-west Pacific, but it was not over yet.

1945 was a year of mixed feeling. Prime Minister Curtin was very ill. On 7 May 1945 the Allies secured victory in Europe. Curtin was too sick to make the announcement to the Australian public so acting Prime Minister Ben Chifley did. Australians were overjoyed but this was balanced against the knowledge that the war was yet to be won in the Pacific.

Curtin died peacefully in his sleep on 5 July. He was 60. There was great sadness as he was a much respected leader who had seen Australia through very dark days. Ben Chifley became Prime Minister.

Two of the crew of the midget submarine I-22. Lieutenant Keiu Matsuo (right) had his head shaved before boarding by First Lieutenant Fujisawa. (Australian War Memorial Negative Number 128889)

On 6 August 1945, a United States aircraft dropped the first atomic bomb on Hiroshima and a second was dropped on Nagasaki on 9 August. On 15 August 1945 Prime Minister Chifley announced the surrender of Japan to the Australian people. This time Australians were exuberant. In the cities, people streamed out into the streets to celebrate with singing and dancing. The next two days were declared public holidays. There was little ethical debate over the dropping of the atomic bombs on Japan. People were just glad the war was over. Many may have felt that the bombs were simply bigger versions of the bombs used on other civilian targets during the war.

When the excitement of the end of the war abated, serious issues had to be considered. Rationing and shortages continued. There were other problems to be tackled as well.

The Government was keen to create a different kind of society in Australia after the war. Already in 1943 a National Welfare Fund was established to provide social security benefits. Unemployment, sickness, hospital benefits and other improvements in social welfare began to be put in place through legislation aimed at providing jobs. Public works schemes were put into motion to provide jobs.

In 1945 another tax, the Social Service Contribution Tax, was introduced to continue the welfare schemes already in existence and to cover the cost of new programmes to assist returned service men and women and their families.

Demobilisation of the approximately 600 000 serving troops began in October 1945 (993 000 in total served during the war). The order of demobilisation depended on the man's age, length of service and family. On their return to Australia and civilian life, service men and women received career advice and information about available housing, employment, repatriation and retraining. Servicemen and women were eligible for a monetary 'bonus'. Cheap war service housing was made available. There were housing short-

Former Japanese prisoner of war members of the 8th Division, Australian Infantry Forces, arrived by Catalina Flying Boat at Rose Bay, Sydney on 16 September 1945. Cheering crowds welcomed them along the route as they travelled by buses to 113th General Hospital for their medical examination. (Australian War Memorial Negative Number 115982)

ages as the return of so many troops boosted the number of those looking for homes.

Women in particular faced some upheaval after the war. Many were now forced to give up their jobs as the servicemen returned home and munitions factories closed down. Others faced widowhood and loneliness. Others found that their husbands were changed men and some suffered divorces and separations due to the war. Some women had to look after wounded or permanently disabled husbands.

The returning troops also faced great adjustments as they tried to return to their normal pre-war civilian lives.

The end of the war marked the realisation of the horrors suffered by inmates of concentration and prisoner of war camps. Many Australian families had to wait to see if loved ones had survived, particularly the 22 000 Australian troops in Japanese prisoners of war camps.

The Government embarked on a mass immigration programme after the war. At that time Australia's population was approximately 7 million and it was clear that Australia needed a larger population for future strength, security and continued economic growth. The Second World War had also created millions of refugees and the Government was compassionate with respect to their plight.

Though the end of the Second World War ushered in peace and the promise of security for Australians, there would be more challenges and battles to be fought in the coming years.

The Legacy of the Second World War —Its Long Term Effect on Australia

Australia suffered 39 366 military deaths and 735 civilian deaths in the war.

- The Federal Government increased in power and prestige.
- The war promoted industrial and technological change.
- Government benefits were given to promote the fields of science and research, exposed as weak during the war.
- Australia became more independent of Britain and strengthened ties with the United States.
- A huge influx of migrants began to arrive.
- Hatred of the Japanese.
- Expansion of social services (welfare).
- The economy stimulated and a manufacturing sector began to develops.
- Partial liberation of women.

The repatriation of nearly 3 000 Japanese prisoners of war began. The Japanese were jeered lustily with boos and hisses as they embarked on the Japanese repatriation ship Daikai Maru Osaka. *This was the first Japanese ship to enter Sydney Harbour since the commencement of hostilities.* (Australian War Memorial Negative Number 126102)